HAL•LEONARD INSTRUMENTAL PLAY-ALONG

CLASSICAL SOLOS FOR BARITONE T.C.
VOLUME 2

ONLINE MEDIA INCLUDED
Audio Recordings
Printable Piano Accompaniments

PLAYBACK+
Speed • Pitch • Balance • Loop

T0081556

To access recordings and PDF accompaniments, visit:
www.halleonard.com/mylibrary
Enter Code
8322-7063-5781-2431

ISBN 978-1-4803-5125-7

HAL•LEONARD®

Visit Hal Leonard Online at
www.halleonard.com

Contact us:
Hal Leonard
7777 West Bluemound Road
Milwaukee, WI 53213
Email: info@halleonard.com

In Europe, contact:
Hal Leonard Europe Limited
42 Wigmore Street
Marylebone, London, W1U 2RN
Email: info@halleonardeurope.com

In Australia, contact:
Hal Leonard Australia Pty. Ltd.
4 Lentara Court
Cheltenham, Victoria, 3192 Australia
Email: info@halleonard.com.au

LARGO
from *Xerxes*

GEORGE FRIDERIC HANDEL
Arranged by PHILIP SPARKE

BARITONE T.C.

Largo (♩ = 68)

Slower

SONGS MY MOTHER TAUGHT ME

from *Gypsy Songs*

BARITONE T.C.

ANTONÍN DVOŘÁK
Arranged by PHILIP SPARKE

MINUET NO. 2
from *Notebook for Anna Magdalena Bach*

Attributed to **CHRISTIAN PEZOLD**
Arranged by PHILIP SPARKE

BARITONE T.C.

00121147

LA CINQUANTAINE
from *Two Pieces for Cello and Piano*

JEAN GABRIEL-MARIE
Arranged by PHILIP SPARKE

BARITONE T.C.

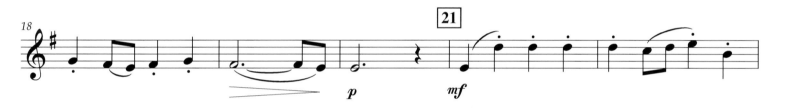

SEE, THE CONQUERING HERO COMES

from *Judas Maccabeus*

GEORGE FRIDERIC HANDEL
Arranged by PHILIP SPARKE

BARITONE T.C.

Allegro (♩ = 132)

SONATINA
Op. 36, No. 1

MUZIO CLEMENTI
Arranged by PHILIP SPARKE

BARITONE T.C.

Allegro (♩ = 88)

SERENATA
from *String Quartet, Op. 3, No. 5*

FRANZ JOSEPH HAYDN
Arranged by PHILIP SPARKE

BARITONE T.C.

Andante cantabile (♩ = 96)

TAMBOURIN
from *Second Suite in E Minor*

BARITONE T.C.

JEAN-PHILIPPE RAMEAU
Arranged by PHILIP SPARKE

00121147

WALTZ
from *Album for the Young*

PYOTR ILYICH TCHAIKOVSKY
Arranged by PHILIP SPARKE

BARITONE T.C.

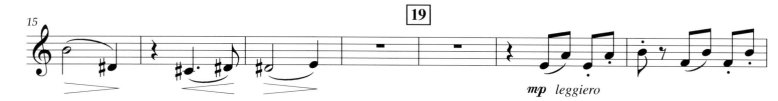

SONATINA

from *Six Pieces, Op. 3*

CARL MARIA VON WEBER
Arranged by PHILIP SPARKE

BARITONE T.C.

Moderato e con amore
(♩ = 120)

GAVOTTE
from *Paride ed Elena*

CHRISTOPH GLUCK/arr. JOHANNES BRAHMS
Arranged by PHILIP SPARKE

BARITONE T.C.

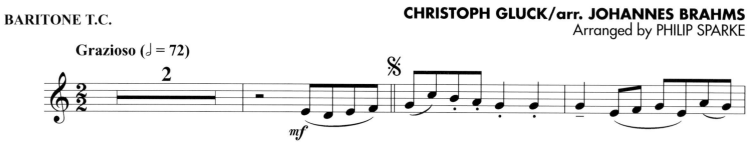

SONATA
Op. 118, No. 1

ROBERT SCHUMANN
Arranged by PHILIP SPARKE

BARITONE T.C.

00121147

SERENADE
from *Schwanengesang, D.957*

BARITONE T.C.

FRANZ SCHUBERT
Arranged by PHILIP SPARKE

SONATINA
Anh. 5, No. 1

LUDWIG VAN BEETHOVEN
Arranged by PHILIP SPARKE

BARITONE T.C.

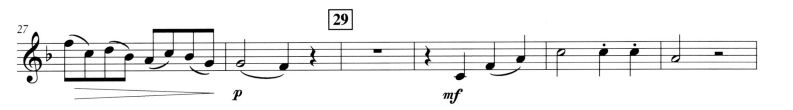

BOURRÉE
from *Flute Sonata, HWV 363b*

BARITONE T.C.

GEORGE FRIDERIC HANDEL
Arranged by PHILIP SPARKE

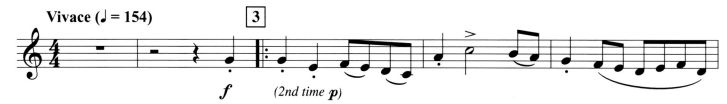